BECKHAM

UNAUTHORISED AND UNOFFICIAL

ENGLAND'S HERO

This is a Parragon Book
First Published in 2004

Parragon, Queen Street House, 4 Queen Street, Bath BAI IHE, UK

ISBN I-40543-232-2

Text written by Julian Flanders
Designed by designsection
All pictures supplied by EMPICS, except page 6 Rex Features and page I6 (centre) Reuters
Printed in China

Contents

From Chase Lane Park to the Bernabeu

It's a long way from Chase Lane Park to the Bernabeu. But both places have one thing in common: David Beckham. Chase Lane Park was just around the corner from the Beckhams' house in Chingford and it was there that David's dad taught him the skills that he now uses each week at the Bernabeu, home of Real Madrid, one of the most famous football clubs in the world.

There's a world of difference too between Ridgeway Rovers, David's first team, who'd turn out each week to play in front of assorted mums and dads, and Real Madrid, who walk out in front of 75,000 fanatic fans to do battle for the honour of the Spanish capital. But as David says, 'For all that so much has happened in my life – and the shirt I'm wearing is a different colour – some things haven't really changed at all.'

Even as a three-year-old, David was always playing football. His dad, Ted, encouraged him. Ted would take him up to nearby Chase Lane Park and spend hours teaching him all the skills: how to trap the ball, how to control it, how to kick it properly and so on. Though he was keen on all sports, representing Chingford High School at swimming, David learned ball skills quickly and for the shy, small, skinny youngster, football gave him the confidence he lacked.

Aged seven David joined his first team, Ridgeway Rovers, a boys' team but one run by people who took their football seriously. They played in local leagues and in competitions in Holland and Germany. Playing for the team all but took over David's life for six years, and he was talented, so talented that people had begun to notice.

Though his dad was a Manchester United fan and encouraged David to follow suit, it was seeing Bryan Robson playing for United in the No.7 shirt that really did it for him. Once hooked, he could not let go, and from then on the Red Devils became his first love.

One day, when David was 10, he saw a report on the BBC's *Blue Peter* about a soccer skills course at Bobby Charlton's Soccer School in Manchester. He applied, got accepted and completed the course successfully. The following year, he attended again and this time entered a competition at the end of the course. The competition was held on the pitch at Old Trafford before a match with Spurs. There were some 40,000 people in the ground and for the youngsters it must have been a thrilling experience. David won the tournament, it was his first taste of glory and, of course, he wanted more.

David's ties with United did not end there. Of course they had noticed him, they had even asked him to be their mascot for an away game at West Ham.

Eventually, Alex Ferguson rang David's dad to ask the youngster up for a trial. For David it was the first contact with a man who would be the driving force behind his career. The trials went well and on 8 July 1991 David signed on with United as a trainee.

Success was not slow in coming. With David in the side, United won the Youth Cup in 1992. A few months later, David made his first-team debut in a League Cup match at Brighton. Though nothing much happened for a while David was shocked in the spring of 1995 when the manager told him that he was being put out on loan to Preston North End. Shocked or not, David went off with good grace. He played five matches for the Third Division side. Then, just as suddenly as he had arrived, he was off again, back to Old Trafford and into the first team for his home debut against Leeds United. It was the start of better things.

David's career at Manchester United was all he had ever dreamed of and more. He became almost a fixture in the team list from 1995. United won the league and FA Cup double the following year, they won six

David Beckham
PERSONAL FACT FILE

NAME: DAVID ROBERT JOSEPH BECKHAM
BORN: LEYTONSTONE, LONDON, 2 MAY 1975
HAIR: LIGHT BROWN
EYES: BLUE
HEIGHT: 5FT 11IN (180CM)
WEIGHT: 10ST 8LB (67KG)
FAMILY: VICTORIA ADAMS; TWO SONS, BROOKLYN, ROMEO
AWARDS WON: PFA YOUNG PLAYER OF THE YEAR 1997; BBC SPORTS PERSONALITY OF THE YEAR 2001; OBE 2003

championships in eight years and they won the Premiership, the FA Cup and the Champions League in 1999. David's skills, his running, his crosses, his free-kicks and his all round ability made him a favourite with United fans. He had started a love affair

David Beckham
MANCHESTER UNITED FACT FILE 1992-2003

SHIRT NO: 7
GAMES PLAYED: 266
GOALS SCORED: 61
HONOURS WON:
CHAMPIONS LEAGUE 1999
PREMIER LEAGUE 1996, 1997, 1999, 2000, 2001, 2003; FA CUP 1996, 1999;
CHARITY SHIELD 1996, 1997

with Old Trafford that saw him become the most famous footballer on the planet.

Maybe that's where things started to go wrong. David's off-the-field activities became as important as his football when he started dating Victoria Adams (aka Posh Spice) in 1997. Their wedding the following year saw media interest in the couple reach a kind of hysteria which remains in place today. His presence in the United team was thought by some to overshadow its performance. During the season 2002–03 Beckham's form dipped. He was dropped from the team amid rumours of a rift with Sir Alex Ferguson. After a dismal FA Cup defeat at home to Arsenal, an angry Sir Alex kicked a stray boot across the room. It hit David in the face, causing a wound that needed a couple of stitches. Although David refused to make a big deal of the incident, the newspapers had other ideas. Rumours grew. Matters came to a head when United lost to Real Madrid in the Champions League quarter-final. Despite coming off the bench and scoring twice to lead a spirited fightback, pictures of Sir Alex dismissing David's efforts were seen on TV that night.

After three or four weeks of feverish speculation, rumours of moves to Milan, Barcelona and others, Real Madrid announced that they had bought David Beckham for a reported £25 million in June 2003. The most famous footballer on earth was joining the most famous football club in the world: it was a marriage made in heaven.

England's Captain Fantastic

With David playing well for the most successful club in the country it was inevitable that he would be called up for England. Though he had been in various Under-18 and Under-19 squads, David Beckham did not win international honours until September 1996 when manager Glenn Hoddle selected him for a World Cup qualifier against Moldova. It was the start of something big. England won the match 3-0 and David retained his place for the rest of the campaign, which ended happily as England got the point they needed to qualify for the finals from a 0-0 draw in the last group match against Italy in Rome.

David had been performing well for his country but in the build up to the World Cup finals in France in 1998 Hoddle hinted that he had doubts about the talented youngster's commitment and temperament and

that Beckam lacked focus. These doubts meant that he left David out of the team for the first match against Tunisia which England won 2-0. Beckham came on as a substitute for Paul Ince during the second match against Romania, but England lost 2-1. Needing to win the final match against Colombia to qualify for the knockout stages, Hoddle included David in the starting line-up, looking to him to produce something special.

Of course, in true David Beckham style, he did produce something – his first goal for England. A free-kick, over the wall and into the net. It was a marvellous moment for David, one in the eye for the doubters and England were through to the next round.

For 23-year-old David Beckham, England v Argentina in the World Cup was one of the biggest games he had ever played in. Chosen to start by Hoddle, along with Michael Owen, it was a night of high drama. Level at 2-2 after the first half and England felt the match was there for the taking. But a few moments later and David's world caved in. After a tussle with Argentina's Diego Simeone, which left David on the ground, David flicked his leg out and Simeone went down in agony, 'acting like he's in intensive care'. The referee did not hesitate and showed David the red card. It was a disaster. Despite a magnificent performance from ten men, England eventually lost on penalties and went out of the tournament.

Over the next few weeks, David suffered at the hands of the manager, the press and the fans as he was blamed for England's World Cup defeat. The headlines were horrid, Hoddle's comments didn't help and David Beckham endured the worst few weeks of his career during the late summer and early autumn of 1998.

It was perhaps during those next few weeks that David grew up. The reaction to his sending off was huge. Opposing fans taunted him with angry words and songs. He became the scapegoat for England's failure. Helped by Sir Alex Ferguson, who gave the player his full support, David knuckled down, trained hard and did his best to turn things around. He got his place back in the England starting line-up after a couple of games and helped the team qualify for the European Championships in Belgium and Holland in 2000. By this time, Hoddle had been replaced in the hot seat by Kevin Keegan for whom David was an automatic choice for a place in the starting line-up. But the tournament turned out to be a bit of a disaster as England lost to Portugal and Romania and, despite a 1-0 win over Germany, were eliminated from the tournament at the first stage. More headlines followed the Portugal match when fans taunted David and he responded with a gesture that was splashed all over the front pages. It was the end of a long and low period for David and for England.

Kevin Keegan resigned soon after Euro 2000 when England lost a World Cup qualifier against Germany in the last match ever staged at the old Wembley. Caretaker manager Peter Taylor was only in charge for one match but asked David to lead the side in a friendly against Italy. It was a defining moment in David's life. Having worked so hard to get himself back in the fold after his sending off, this was the culmination of his efforts. Confirmation of the wisdom of this move came when the newly appointed Sven-Goran Eriksson confirmed that David would continue as captain. And as England started to improve, so did David's form, his influence and his abilities as a captain.

A magnificent performance in the return match against Germany resulted in a crushing 5-1 win in Munich in one of the England team's finest performances ever. But more drama was yet to come. England needed a point from the final match to ensure qualification.
The match was at home to Greece and was to be played at Old Trafford. It turned out to be Beckham's match. In a generally drab performance,

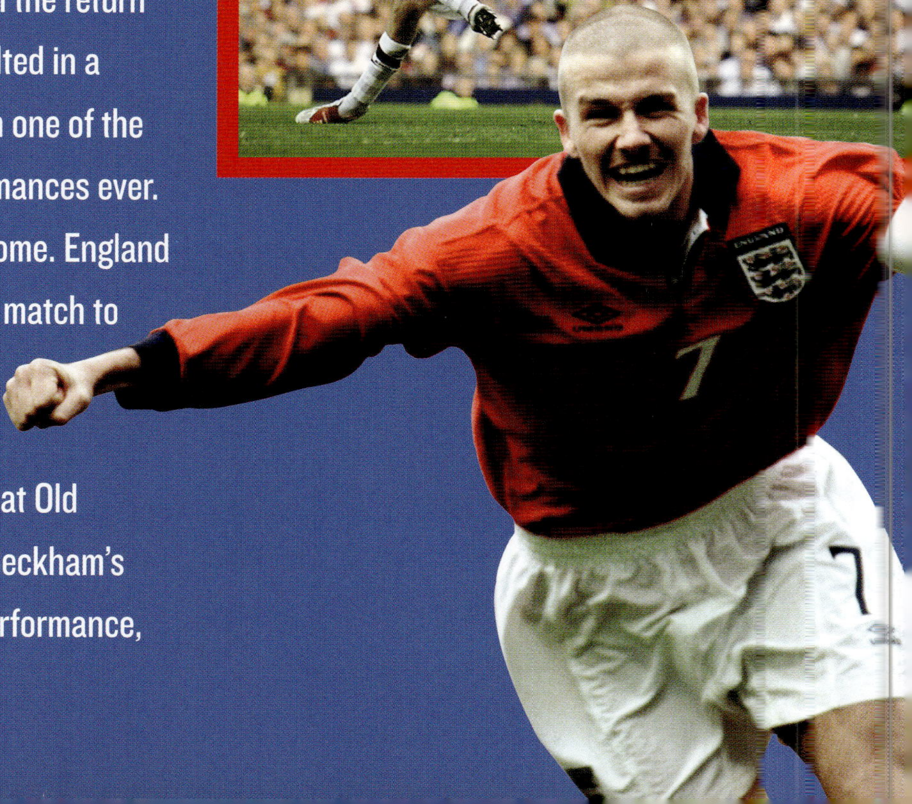

David was immense, tackling, passing, running, directing the whole game. With a minute left, England trailed 2-1, but they won a free-kick just outside the Greek penalty area. David placed the ball, stepped back and looked up. The crowd went quiet. He stepped up, cheeks puffed out and struck the ball. It arced sweetly over the wall and slapped into the back of the net. Old Trafford went wild. With the last kick of the match, the captain had scored on his home ground and England were in the World Cup finals. He had played a true captain's role, the sort of thing that only happens in dreams.

The hysteria surrounding England's 2002 World Cup campaign grew to epic proportions. David was injured playing for Manchester United a few weeks before the tournament started and for a while it was touch and go whether he would be fit or not. In the end, he was just about fit enough to make the trip to Japan and Korea and how England needed him. Mobbed by ecstatic fans wherever he went, David still kept his mind on the job. After a draw in the first match against Sweden, England had to play old foes Argentina. England's determination to get revenge for 1998 was obvious as the match got underway. Half way through the first

half, England were awarded a penalty after Michael Owen was brought down in the area. David grabbed the ball and put it down on the spot. It was another defining moment in his footballing career. He got good contact on the ball and it flew into the net passed a flat-footed keeper and England were 1-0 ahead. One dragon had been slayed.

The victory ensured that England qualified for the knockout stages. They beat Denmark 3-0 in the next round to set up a quarter-final with Brazil. A goal by Michael Owen gave England the lead and raised the hopes of the nation. But an equaliser from Rivaldo and a bizarre free-kick from Ronaldinho that went over David Seaman's head ensured that Brazil made it to the semis. At the end of the match the disappointment on David's face said it all. However, England had reached the last eight and had performed creditably.

It is no coincidence that David's rise in stature as a player and as the captain of the national team has happened during Sven-Goran Eriksson's time as England coach. Sven knows his captain well, giving him space for his family life, supporting him and trusting him to lead the team by example. David has responded perfectly and is now able to face the press, deal with criticism and perform to the highest level on the pitch. It's quite an achievement for a small, shy lad from Chingford, who was regarded as too frail to make the grade as a footballer.

But it can never be said of David that he is a shrinking violet. England's route to the European Championships finals in Portugal in 2004 was fraught with danger. Most notably from Turkey, a team who had finished third in the 2002 World Cup and who many regarded as one of the favourites. The two teams were neck and neck, trading victories against the other teams in the group. When they met at the Stadium of Light in Sunderland, England played well and won 2-0. David scored a last-minute penalty to put icing on the cake. But there was trouble on the pitch and Turkey left promising revenge during the return match.

Still the two teams were locked together at the top of the qualifying group table. The final match of the group was to be played in Istanbul. Amid fears of violence, England fans were not allowed to travel and so the team went alone to face 50,000 fanatic supporters needing a point to win the group. Despite provocation, intimidation and missing a first-half penalty, David steered England towards the point they needed. It was another massive performance from England's Captain Fantastic.

David Beckham
ENGLAND FACT FILE 1996–2003

SHIRT NO: 7

GAMES PLAYED: 65*

GOALS SCORED: 13*

* figures correct as of 1 January 2004

Bernabeu Boy

When it finally happened, it wasn't a surprise that David left Old Trafford. It was time for him to go. There was little more he could win with United and relations with Sir Alex Ferguson were not at their best. Besides, who could turn down the chance to play at the Santiago Bernabeu – one of the most famous stadiums in the world – alongside some of the finest players in the world?

However, the furore surrounding the transfer and the Beckhams' arrival in the Spanish capital was immense. David and his family travelled to Spain on the last day of June 2003.

A successful medical, sponsored by a pharmaceutical company and shown live on Spanish TV, was followed by David officially signing his contract. His introduction to the press and the fans followed the next day. The ceremony was held at the Pabellon Raimondo Saporta, a 5,000-seater basketball arena in the Real Madrid training complex. On the stage with David was Alfredo di Stefano, for many the best player the world has ever seen, and Florentino Perez, President of Real Madrid. Di Stefano held the famous shirt of Real Madrid. He shook hands with David and together they held out the shirt for all to see, they turned it around to reveal the number 23 and the legend 'Beckham'.

After the press conference, David paraded his skills for photographers. Thousands of fans had turned up to welcome him. One young fan, oblivious to the security guards, ran onto the pitch. David saw him, waved the security men away and hugged him. David managed to get hold of a second shirt to give to the boy. It was a marvellous moment. With that gesture, David ensured that many of the Real fans would take him immediately to their hearts.

A few days after he had signed for Real, the team left Spain on a promotional tour to China and Hong Kong. David and his team-mates were welcomed by thousands of fans wherever they went. Training sessions were attended by the world's press and interest in the various matches was huge. It was a great opportunity for David to get used to playing with his new team. The tour was a great success in many ways.

The football was good, David scored his first goal for his new club in the match against FC Tokyo, hundreds of thousands of Beckham's shirts were sold and Real Madrid's reputation as the most famous football club in the world was enhanced. David returned from the tour ready to face the challenges of life in a new country and football with a new club in a new and fantastically skilful league. It was just the challenge he needed.

SUNTORY SUNTORY
SIEMENS mobile

Domestically, the season started well for David and for Real Madrid. They won the Spanish Super Cup, beating Real Mallorca. David obliged with a goal in the second leg in front of his new fans at the Bernabeu. Their early league form was good too, and even the doubters could see that David was making quite an impression with his football.

It was not long before David revealed that he was pleased with his form and that his skills had already improved through playing with Real's 'galacticos'. He said, 'When you play with great players, you can only learn from them. Even in training, there are things you can take from the likes of Zinedine Zidane, Luis Figo, Ronaldo, Roberto Carlos and Raul'.

Raul was the first of the old guard to respond when he said, 'Beckham is a great player, an ace. He has proved [that] in every match since the start of the season. He has earned his place in our team'. Luis Figo agreed, 'Beckham has definitely made us stronger than last year. He's doing very well. It always takes time to integrate yourself into a new club and a new town, with a new language too. But I think he has improved already because his mind is open to want to get better.'

A few months into his career as a Real Madrid player Beckham still had a few things to learn about life at the Bernabeu. Real is a unique club, one where ultimate glory only comes with silverware. Regular league or cup victories are hardly celebrated at all. After all, winning is normal for Real. Glory finishes when the match ends. It is said that there is no other team where happiness escapes so quickly. The failure of defeat, however, is remembered until the next game.

Despite this, a victory sees Beckham emerge from the dressing room with a broad grin. He is keen to share his joy with the press and with his friends. His spectacular goal against Albacete in November, the first in a 2-1 victory that saw Real go to the top of the table for the first time during the season, saw a jubilant Beckham at the press conference. He was typically understated when asked about his stunning 25-yard shot, 'I was pleased with it,' he said. 'It was nice for me to score another one which was not from a set-piece'.

But for now Beckham is taking his life in Spain very seriously. On arrival at the Bernabeu, he was told by Real's Director of Football Jorge Valdano that he had to learn Spanish as soon as possible. Valdano was keen that Beckham settle in quickly and that he learned about the particular idiosyncrasies of the club. Of course, language books were provided

and lessons were arranged immediately. Brazilian teammate Roberto Carlos has also taught Beckham words that he clearly uses during games. Though he is not particularly garrulous on the training ground or in the changing room, Beckham surprised everyone one weekday after training in November when he replied to a question about his fitness from Real's Press Officer Paco Navacerrada, 'Estoy bien,' he said, 'muy bien, puedo jugar perfectamente' ('I'm well, very well, I am able to play perfectly').

There is no doubt now that Beckham did the right thing moving to Spain. His fame has brought happiness to Real Madrid and his football has benefited from his new colleagues and his new training regime. So central is he to the team that it is almost as though he has played there all his life. With Real heading the Spanish league table and remaining favourites for the Champions League and with England ready to take part in Euro 2004 there seems no limit to what David Beckham can achieve.

David Beckham

REAL MADRID FACT FILE 2003–

SHIRT NO: 23

GAMES PLAYED: 20*

GOALS SCORED: 5*

* figures correct as of I January 2004

QUIZ

So now you've read the book, how much do you know about David Beckham? Here's a quiz that'll sort you out.

FIRST HALF

1. When was David born?
2. In which district of which city was he born?
3. How old was he when he signed on as a apprentice with Manchester United in 199 ?
4. Against which team did he make his first-team debut for Manchester United in 1992?
5. David played five games on loan to which Third Division club in 1995?
6. In 1996 David scored a wonder goal from the halfway line against which London club?
7. Against which team did David make his England debut?
8. Against which team did David score his first goal for England?
9. Which England manager first gave David the captain's armband?
10. Against which team did David first captain his country?

HALF-TIME SCORE

FULL-TIME SCORE

INSTRUCTIONS: Toss a coin to decide who's playing at 'home'. Home player goes first. You get a goal for each correct answer. There are ten questions in the first half and ten questions in the second half. If the scores are level at the end, then there's a Golden Goal question to decide who wins. If you have to look up the answers in the book, then you get a yellow card. If you look up the answers on the next page, then you get a red card and you lose the game. So be careful.

SECOND HALF

11 Which player did David kick to get himself sent off in the 1998 World Cup finals?

12 David scored a penalty against which country in the 2002 World Cup?

13 Against which team did David make his last appearance for Manchester United?

14 How many Premiership titles did David win with Manchester United?

15 In which month of which year was David transferred to Real Madrid?

16 What number does David wear on his Real Madrid shirt?

17 What is the name of Real Madrid's ground?

18 Who is David's favourite pop star?

19 One of David's team-mates at Real Madrid is the world's most expensive footballer. What is his name?

20 Against which team did David score his first goal in La Liga?

GOLDEN GOAL QUESTION

Only to be used if the scores are level (first person to shout the correct answer wins the game)

What are David Beckham's two middle names?

QUIZ ANSWERS

1 2 May 1975
2 Leytonstone, London
3 16
4 Brighton
5 Preston North End
6 Wimbledon
7 Moldova
8 Colombia
9 Peter Taylor
10 Italy
11 Diego Simeone
12 Argentina
13 Everton
14 6
15 June 2003
16 23
17 The Bernabeu
18 Usher
19 Zinedine Zidane (who cost £45.8 million)
20 Real Betis

Golden Goal: **Robert and Joseph**